Birds of Prey
of the Midwest

Stan Tekiela

Adventure Quick Guides
YOUR WAY TO EASILY IDENTIFY RAPTORS

Birds of Prey Identification Guide

This guide includes all 34 raptor species found in the Midwest. Use these general characteristics to help identify the group, and then turn to the thumb tab.

EAGLES
- enormous wingspans of 6–8'
- slow, powerful wing beats
- glide with wings straight at body level

HAWKS
- wide wings
- flap, then glide
- circle up, then soar

OSPREY
- angled wings
- fast, shallow wing beats
- plunges into water feet first for fish

FALCONS
- long, tapered wings
- agile, rapid flight
- hover, dive and glide

KITES
- pointed wings
- buoyant, bouncy flight with long glides
- swoop to feed on insects while flying

VULTURES
- spreading wing tips
- teetering flight with wings in a slight V
- small naked heads

OWLS
- large heads, thick bodies
- eyes in front of face
- short tails

Eagles

Golden Eagle

golden nape,
female larger,
with longer wings

WS - 7' **L** - 33"

adult

juvenile

adult

juvenile

Bald Eagle

white head and tail,
female larger, with
longer wings

WS - 7' **L** - 34"

adult

juvenile

adult

juvenile

Golden Eagle

Bald Eagle

Sharp-shinned Hawk

bluish gray back, small head, squared tail, female gray back

WS - 2' L - 11"

male

juvenile

female

adult

juvenile

Cooper's Hawk

large head, small eyes, rounded tail

WS - 2½' L - 16"

adult

juvenile

adult

juvenile

Sharp-shinned Hawk

Cooper's Hawk

Broad-winged Hawk

rusty brown bib, black and white tail bands

WS - 2¾' **L** - 17"

adult

adult

Red-shouldered Hawk

rust-to-orange barring on chest and belly

WS - 3½' **L** - 17"

adult

adult

Broad-winged Hawk

Red-shouldered Hawk

Northern Harrier

white rump, long tail, facial disk, female brown

male

female

WS - 3½'   L - 18"

male

female

Northern Goshawk

gray with white line above eyes

WS - 3½'   L - 21"

adult

juvenile

adult

juvenile

Northern Harrier

Northern Goshawk

Hawks

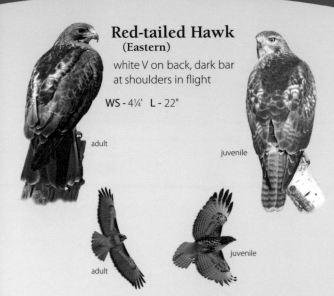

Red-tailed Hawk
(Eastern)

white V on back, dark bar
at shoulders in flight

WS - 4¼'   L - 22"

adult

juvenile

adult

juvenile

Red-tailed Hawk
(Krider's)

white head and
chest, pale tail, lacks
belly band

WS - 4¼'   L - 22"

adult

adult

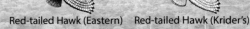

Red-tailed Hawk (Eastern)   Red-tailed Hawk (Krider's)

Red-tailed Hawk
(Western)

dark chin, heavily
streaked belly

WS - 4¼' **L** - 22"

adult

adult

juvenile

Red-tailed Hawk (Harlan's)

dark with white flecking,
lacks red tail

WS - 4¼' **L** - 22"

adult

adult

Red-tailed Hawk (Western)

Red-tailed Hawk (Harlan's)

Rough-legged Hawk (light)

wide dark belly band, dark wrist patches in flight

WS - 4½' L - 20"

adult

adult

juvenile

Rough-legged Hawk (dark)

overall dark brown to nearly black, small bill

WS - 4½' L - 20"

adult

adult

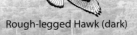

Rough-legged Hawk (light)   Rough-legged Hawk (dark)

Hawks

Swainson's Hawk
(light)

rusty bib,
dark trailing
wing edges
in flight, female
brown bib

male

female

WS - 4½' L - 20"

adult

juvenile

Swainson's Hawk
(dark)

dark brown with
yellow between
eyes and bill

WS - 4½' L - 20"

adult

adult

juvenile

Swainson's Hawk (light)   Swainson's Hawk (dark)

Rough-legged Hawk (light)

wide dark belly band, dark wrist patches in flight

WS - 4½' L - 20"

adult

adult

juvenile

Rough-legged Hawk (dark)

overall dark brown to nearly black, small bill

WS - 4½' L - 20"

adult

adult

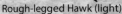

Rough-legged Hawk (light)

Rough-legged Hawk (dark)

Swainson's Hawk
(light)

rusty bib,
dark trailing
wing edges
in flight, female
brown bib

male

female

WS - 4½' L - 20"

adult

juvenile

Swainson's Hawk
(dark)

dark brown with
yellow between
eyes and bill

WS - 4½' L - 20"

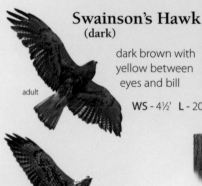

adult

adult

juvenile

Swainson's Hawk (light)   Swainson's Hawk (dark)

Hawks

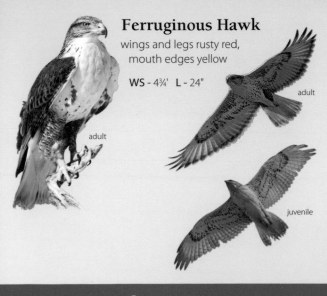

Ferruginous Hawk

wings and legs rusty red,
mouth edges yellow

WS - 4¾' **L -** 24"

adult

adult

juvenile

Osprey

Osprey

dark eye stripe,
white body,
female neck-
lace mark

adult

adult

WS - 5¼' **L -** 23"

Ferruginous Hawk

Osprey

Merlin
(Taiga)

blue back, heavily
marked chest,
female brown back

WS - 1¾' L - 11"

male

juvenile

female

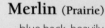

adult

juvenile

Merlin (Prairie)

blue back, heavily
marked chest

WS - 1¾' L - 11"

adult

adult

Merlin (Taiga)

Merlin (Prairie)

Falcons

American Kestrel

dark vertical lines on face, female brown wings

WS - 1¾' L - 11"

male

juvenile

female

male

female

Prairie Falcon

speckled black wing linings, female black wing linings

male

adult

female

WS - 3¼' L - 16"

American Kestrel

Prairie Falcon

Peregrine Falcon

black "hood," pointed
wings in flight

WS - 3½' **L** - 17"

adult

juvenile

adult

juvenile

Gyrfalcon

gray to brown, pointed
wings in flight

WS - 4¼' **L** - 22"

adult

adult

Peregrine Falcon

Gyrfalcon

Kites

Mississippi Kite

overall gray with dark patch around red eyes

WS - 2½' L - 13"

adult

juvenile

adult

juvenile

Swallow-tailed Kite

white with black wings and tail, swallow-like forked tail

WS - 4¼' L - 20"

adult

adult

Mississippi Kite

Swallow-tailed Kite

Black Vulture

short tail, gray-tipped wings, naked gray head

WS - 5' L - 27"

adult

juvenile

adult

Turkey Vulture

teeters in flight, gray trailing wing edges, naked red head

WS - 5¾' L - 29"

adult

juvenile

adult

Black Vulture

Turkey Vulture

Owls

Northern Saw-whet Owl
brown vertical stripes

L - 7"   **WS** - 1½'

Eastern Screech-Owl
short ear tufts, yellow eyes

L - 9"   **WS** - 1¾'

red

gray

Burrowing Owl
long legs, streaked crown, white throat

L - 9"   **WS** - 1¾'

Northern Saw-whet Owl   Eastern Screech-Owl   Burrowing Owl

Boreal Owl

white-to-gray face, white spots

L - 10" **WS** - 1½'

Long-eared Owl

long ear tufts, rusty face

L - 15" **WS** - 2¾'

Northern Hawk Owl

long narrow pointed tail

L - 16" **WS** - 2½'

Boreal Owl

Long-eared Owl

Northern Hawk Owl

Short-eared Owl

dark patch around eyes, tiny ear tufts

L - 16" **WS** - 3¼'

Barn Owl

heart-shaped white face, female rusty chest and belly

L - 17" **WS** - 3¼'

male

female

Barred Owl

large body, dark eyes

L - 22" **WS** - 3¼'

Short-eared Owl

Barn Owl

Barred Owl

Owls

Great Horned Owl
large ear tufts, yellow eyes

L - 23" **WS** - 3¾'

Snowy Owl
white with yellow eyes,
female dark marks

L - 23" **WS** - 5'

male

female

Great Gray Owl
large head, small yellow eyes

L - 27" **WS** - 4¼'

Great Horned Owl

Snowy Owl

Great Gray Owl